AF211646

JEROLD ELEANOR

SECRETS OF DIVINE LOVE

The Ultimate Guide to Spiritual Living and Healing, Discover the Steps and Best Practices on How to Live a Spiritually-Fulfilled Life

Descrierea CIP a Bibliotecii Naționale a României
JEROLD ELEANOR
   SECRETS OF DIVINE LOVE. The Ultimate Guide to Spiritual Living and Healing, Discover the Steps and Best Practices on How to Live a Spiritually-Fulfilled Life / Jerold Eleanor – Bucharest: Editura My Ebook, 2021
   ISBN

JEROLD ELEANOR

SECRETS OF DIVINE LOVE
The Ultimate Guide to Spiritual Living and Healing, Discover the Steps and Best Practices on How to Live a Spiritually-Fulfilled Life

My Ebook Publishing House
Bucharest, 2021

TABLE OF CONTENTS

INTRODUCTION

Whether you participate in a popular faith or take an independent course, whether you trust in divine creation or cling to stern physical objectivity, your notions about truth define the overall context of your life. In this sense, all of us are spiritual beings as we all have certain beliefs about truth. Even to trust nothing might still be considered part of a spiritual belief system.

Your spiritual growth is a built-in part of the process of human development. Truth, affection, and major power don't prescribe a certain spiritual doctrine, so there's lots of freedom to research a mixture of beliefs. However, the highest ideal for your spiritual doctrine is becoming intelligent.

If your beliefs don't fulfill the necessities of being intelligent at the very least, they can't be thought spiritually sound as they'd be in violation of universal principles. If a spiritual doctrine yields to untruth, if it disconnects you from life, or if it breaks you, it infringes on the rules and will only lead you astray.

Social conditioning teaches us to have secure bonds to our spiritual notions to the point of blending such notions into our identities. In this audiobook, I'll challenge you to view your spiritual feelings with truth, affection, and power. My goal isn't to convert you to abide by any particular practice but rather to help you bring greater conscious awareness to your current spiritual life.

CHAPTER 1

WHAT IT MEANS TO LIVE
SPIRITUALLY FULFILLED

Synopsis

Being happy is often misinterpreted in many ways. Most of the ways that the feeling of happiness is derived from is really not the product of true happiness but only a temporal feeling. People associate happiness with things like money, power, achieving dreams and goals, fame, accomplishments, all of which have material connections and bench marks.

The Basics

True happiness is when one in completely at peace mentally and physically in the spiritually fulfilled self. Being able to find contentment anywhere, anytime and in anything is true happiness, and spiritual fulfillment.

In order to live spiritually fulfilled there are certain guidelines or recommendations one can follow. Here are some of them:

- Coming to the realization that one's life has a higher purpose, and that just achieving material goals for short term comforts is understanding that there is more to life than just these tangible things that bring temporal happiness and no lasting spiritual contentment.

This brings on the understanding that each individual has a reason and purpose to be on this earth and finding that purpose should be the focal point of life.

• Spiritual fulfillment is finding the bliss in life. The thing that brings most happiness to the individual and keep it constant in the cycle of everyday life.

• Love life and love the path taken in life. Even if circumstances does not allow one to love every aspect of the task at hand, looking at it with a positive mind set allows the mind to change the thought process from negative to positive, thus successfully transcending the feeling of love and peace which in turn evolves into spiritual fulfillment.

• In growing and expanding both mentally and in terms of capabilities the feeling of boredom or annoyance will be kept at bay. Deriving pleasure from this willingness to explore also bring the feeling of spiritual fulfillment.

CHAPTER 2

WHERE DOES YOUR SPIRITUAL LIFE
NEED HELP

Synopsis

A strong spiritual life entails several facets of a single entity. Being spiritually balanced and fulfilled is when each piece of life's puzzle in firmly in place, understood and happily accepted.

Evaluate

Some of the areas that can benefit from having a balanced and complete spiritual life are to have a strong and firm spiritual support system in place.

The support should come from the surroundings, such as relationships, experiences, prayer and so on. The idea that solitude is the prerequisite of inner peace and spirituality is indeed a folly. Social interactions and experience is crucial to the development spirituality.

Being a loving and responsible individual is the first steps towards spiritual development. People must be able to love and loving unconditionally is even better for spiritual life. The practice of love and its unbound capabilities should not be limited to the inner circle of the people around but should be indiscriminately extended to all.

Advancing to higher levels of spirituality should be the ultimate goal and by loving and serving, the exercise of consistent love for fellow human beings is being nurtured and fulfilled.

Getting the support from people around, like family members and friends, work associated and others is important to achieving a spiritually fulfilled life.

These are the people who will help the individual to grow by the support and good direction provided to keep on track always. Life greatest teachers are those who are willing to step out and help to provide the necessary advice and guidance with no thought for self gain.

Spiritually fulfilled life can be gotten through the energy expounded in relationships. The kindness and boots or awareness for others allows for the "self" element to be least considered and others needs to be addressed.

This energy gained from these experiences and interactions bring about a sense of joy and peace which contributes to achieving spiritual fulfillment.

CHAPTER 3

ENVISION WHAT YOUR LIFE WOULD LOOK LIKE IF YOU WERE WHERE YOU WANT TO BE SPIRITUALLY

Synopsis

Of late there is a lot of information available on the spirituality of a human being. With the chaos around the world and peace an elusive item, people are searching for alternatives to make their lives complete or at the very least better. One of the avenues worth exploring is the spiritual side of life. It has been touted to have wonderfully enlightening effects for both the body and soul.

See It

Being connected spiritually has its benefits. It certainly changes a person for the better. People become more sensitive to what's around them and respond with equal amounts of sensitivity.

This therefore helps the individual to learn to be less self centered and more self giving. This also allows the mind to acknowledge the presence of higher forces that are powerful and all perfect when compared to the human existence.

When spiritually balanced, one also seeks to give love unconditionally. Being focused on giving love unconditionally becomes a central part of the individual. In this ideal setting of giving love, peace is ultimately found.

The willingness to set aside time in this busy and chaotic world is indeed rare, but when spiritual attainment is found, the eagerness to spend time meditating, contemplating or simply just wanting to commune with nature and the surroundings becomes very much a part of the daily routine.

An individual also evolves into a positive character and becomes more accepting as a person. The previous judgmental person is replaced with a more understanding and compassionate disposition. The character trait of graciousness is built and strengthened.

Seeking to forgive the past is also another by product of attaining spirituality. Understanding that un-forgiveness, benefits no one and can be detrimental to health becomes clear. This in turn develops the kindness in a person.

CHAPTER 4

LEARN HOW TO OVERCOME OBSTRUCTIONS TO CHANGING YOUR BEHAVIORS

Synopsis

Most times a wrong situation can be put right immediately and with little problems. However when the element of the human behavior is involved things are not as clear cut and simple. Here are some obstructions that can be successfully addressed with a change in behavior.

Overcome

Learning to become a more accepting person and practicing the ability to adopt easily is one behavioral change that is worth building as this good trait will become an asset in interactions with others.

Another obstruction that can be addressed with a change in behavior and attitude is the ability to forgive and move on easily. Cultivating the positive mind set allows for the feelings of guilt and anger to be released and results in a kinder and gentler demeanor.

The inability to see the good in others is an undesirable behavior pattern that can cause obstructions in both the individual's life and that of those around.

Being quick to judge is not only foolish but also damaging. Changing this negative thinking also subconsciously brings forth the positive thinking of the "can do" attitude that attracts good.

Learning to take stock of the actions meted out daily teaches the individual to learn how to analyze thoughts and reactions that merited the particular action taken and if the action was unmerited and harsh, further steps can be taken to readdress the situation, easily removing the obstructive initial response. This allows the person to grow mentally and spiritually.

Being egoistical can be very destructive in any scenario. This destructive behavior can cause a lot of ill feeling among those directly or indirectly in contact with the egoistical individual. There are many obstructions that can be avoided if this bad behavior trait is changed. Few people can tolerate working or being associated with egoistical people.

CHAPTER 5

CHOOSE YOUR SPIRITUAL GOALS
AND BREAK THEM INTO MANAGEABLE STEPS

Synopsis

The idea that everyone should have specific goals in life is a good idea to live up to. However having goals without any guide lines on how to reach them is indeed foolish. There are several important steps that need to be considered before anyone takes and interest in setting goals. Here are some recommended suggestions.

Deciding

Ideally the first step should be to identify the goal in mind clearly and correctly. Having a vague idea of the goal is quite confusing for the mind to interpret. The human mind is similar to a computer, when specific information is fed; the mind is able to work more efficiently and quickly to produce the necessary results. When the information is unclear as in a vague goal, then the mind works overtime and inefficiently and in the end nothing is accomplished.

When this is done, the next step is to address any previous forays into attempting the goal's success. By doing this it is hoped that any of the same ill maintained styles are eliminated altogether so that new styles can be implemented to try and gain a more successful attempt.

Some of the areas to explore that may cause development in the individual spiritual life are character goals which focus on love issues, patience, and faithfulness. Family goals are also important to explore more in depth where aspects such as how much quality time are spent with spouse and children.

Addressing physical needs are also paramount when trying to choose spiritual goals. The body and mind both need to be in healthy condition before any successful attempt of goal setting can be done. Some specific issues may have to be addressed and dealt with, such as weight problems, lack of stamina, perhaps the need to lose weight and exercise.

CHAPTER 6

SET A DEADLINE FOR EACH SPIRITUAL GOAL

Synopsis

Sometimes people wonder why they are only successful in certain areas while in other areas there seems to be a lot of strife and difficulty. One possible answer could be that they failed to set spiritual goals to help overcome this negative area. A big part of not being able to achieve certain goals is probably because the spiritual guidance and element is missing.

Make A Timeline

Rejoicing in the assurance of God's divine power of deliverance is perhaps what gives the goal that added advantage in being reached. Setting a deadline for spiritual goals is one way of committing our efforts to God and realizing without divine intervention or help reaching the goal would be that much harder if not impossible.

In order to outline a workable deadline setting, it would be wise to break the goal in question into more specific and smaller parts. In denoting the importance of each particular part, a spiritually guided deadline can be set for each step.

Having a measurable scale where each progressive step is recorded and bench marked against the overall planned goal schedule is helpful. When done in unity and understanding upon the power of strength gained with God's assistance this can be achieved well within the time frame matted out. This is an important element because it gives the individual an indication of the success of the goal's progress and also ensures no sense of discouragement sets in.

After addressing the above two points successfully, the next step is to actually implement the action plan drawn up to reach the goal. Making an action plan, while calling on God for spiritual assistance, will not only cause the action plan to be flawless, but will also give the individual the power of spiritual insight.

CHAPTER 7

BRAINSTORM IDEAS TO SPIRITUALITY
OR TALK TO A SPIRITUAL LEADER

Synopsis

Setting goals is an important frame of mind to have, as has already been established in the various other presentations. However if an added advantage is needed to ensure the goal is reached and also to ensure it is for the good of all concerned, turning to spiritual guidance is a prerequisite.

Make A Plan

When an idea is first conceived it may have in most cases been with the goal of achieving some form of earthly element or pleasure.

However if there is the spiritual guidance of a spiritual leader then the danger of the idea being just that, for earthly pleasure, may be checked, rethought or better still shelved altogether. Having the advantage of spiritual elements involved will certainly assure its integrity and success.

A spiritual leader will be able to steer the focus on a more God centered results and methods and in turn this ensures that the goal and people connected to achieving the goal will not work blindly or sinfully.

Also by knowing that there is a percentage of spiritual involvement it gives everyone connected to the goal a sense of divine guidance which is assuredly never wrong.

Spiritual leaders are usually so in tune with God's teachings for the happiness of the human existence that they are able to advice accordingly so all concerned are able to clearly focus on achieving the goal set.

The feelings of cooperation and comradeship will be obvious and every present. Spiritual leaders are able to give specific quotes of God's favor in dire situations and this will help to keep the moral of those involved from in the journey to achieving the goad high and recharged.

With the advice of a spiritual leader, those involved in the goal will also know how to turn to God's when inspiration, innovation and just plain strength is needed to press on to overcome any obstacles that may otherwise hinder the enthusiasm of all.

CHAPTER 8

ASK FOR DEVINE GUIDANCE

Synopsis

Besides the spiritual side of life there is also the practical side of life. Though both are entwined, they are quite different in nature and approach.

People who are spiritually aware will always try to seek out divine revelations or interventions in whatever foray they are a part of. The general perception is, if there is divine intervention then the possibility of any negative presence will be eliminated or controlled and all will be well.

Ask For Help

Some of the questions that can be asked in order to affirm spiritual guidance are as follows:

- Is this in harmony with God's Word?
- Is it what the scripture encourages?
- Does it follow God's rule and will?
- Am I being prompted by the Holy Spirit?
- Would my conduct be in line with God's righteousness?

There is a lot of vagueness and hesitation when embarking on something new, especially if there are a lot of risks involved. Being at peace is a very important feature to have to ensure the smoothness of the foray in question. By practicing the mindset that constantly seeks divine guidance; some of the above hesitations based on the questions can be addressed and answered effectively and clearly. However these answers for guidance can only be gotten when there is a spiritual link that is very strong and sincere.

Most teaching encourage seeking divine guidance for everything in life be it big or small, important or otherwise. When this habit is formed due to frequent practice, the body, and mind become in tuned with the spiritual inner self and thus drawing from this will be easier.

Another popular train of thought is that by seeking divine guidance, there is absolutely no room for error when the guidance is ardently followed. If there are any errors to be found it would be on the side of the individual for not following the divine guidance totally.

CHAPTER 9

REMEMBER THE GOLDEN RULE

Synopsis

Do unto others as you would have it done to you. A very simple yet at the same time a terribly complex statement to adhere to. Most people never stop and think of their actions and how other people on the receiving end feel. In this fast pace world few take the trouble to analyze the repercussions of their works, actions, and thoughts.

Be Kind

In treating others the way one would want to be treated, makes the individual stop and take stock of the words, actions, and mannerism used when interacting with others.

This can be achieved when people slow down and are more spiritually connected with their surroundings. Some would say knowledge and imagination are a prerequisite as there would be the need to imagine being on the receiving end instead of only on the giving out end.

Being able to completely accept the same treatment meted out to others would ensure the individual is more careful and aware of how to conduct his or her everyday life. This will certainly help in shaping the moral thinking of each individual.

Strangely though, the golden rule principle does not really have any particular moral formula. As it is neither right not wrong but is based on the simple theory that "you get what you give" the golden rule phenomenon is actually tapping on the individual desire to receive only good while being fairly sure that extending good is the prerequisite. This rule borders on the fact that most human have the in built self preservation instinct.

Practiced all over the world and in all walks of society, the golden rule principle is adhered to, in order to preserves feelings and relationships better that any other physical or mental practice can do, simply by its non complicated one rule.

CHAPTER 10

WHAT HAPPENS IF YOU
ARE SPIRITUALLY DEPRIVED

Synopsis

Being spiritually deprived leads to a lot of negative problems. Though medical science has over the years acknowledged the advantages of being connected spiritually, people in general have not yet grasped this important tool for their life.

One of the factors that lead to less than optimum mental and physical health of an individual is the lack of spirituality. Being more connected to the secular and materialistic society is one of the contributing factors to the lack of importance placed on spirituality.

What Can Occur

The biggest impact of being spiritually deprived from a medical point of view is the onset of depression. Currently viewed as a very wide spread problem, depression seems to have direct links with the lack of spirituality in an individual's life.

The medical world recognizes this phenomenon as dangerous and growing daily but is unable to adequately endorse the importance between the connection of spirituality and the human body.

When stress levels rise, as they do in this fast moving and unforgiving world it's more often than not to find adequate solutions that are effective and long lasting.

For a long time the question of spirituality and the general connection to the human mind has been questioned. Spiritual enlightenment is central to the unity of body, soul, and mind; however it is unfortunately ignored as the core of the human existence.

CHAPTER 11

WHAT IS SPIRITUAL HEALING

Synopsis

Basically spiritual healing is a method where an individual with healing energy transfers the positive energy from themselves on to the person in need.

This method of positive energy transfer is usually done using the hands of the spiritually filled individual called a healer. However it should be understood at this point, the healing does not come from the healer but though the healer. The healer is just a vessel for the positive energy.

What's Behind It

There are some that believe every individual is capable of tapping into their own personal positive energy for healing purposes. This is done spiritually through prayer. The term spiritual refer to the energy source that is divine in nature and available to all without any discrimination.

Most spiritual healers look upon a health problem as inter connected to the body, mind and spirit. If one part is causing the problem all the other parts must be addressed too because of their close connection in producing the problem in the first place.

Almost all the healers believe that most medical problems start with the state of the mind and these manifests into other symptoms that become evident in a physical form.

Therefore their primary goal is to restore the balance in the entire body system as a way to complete the process of spiritual healing.

This form of treatment is becoming very popular indeed, as it promises a better alternative to invasive medical procedures. There is also a "hunger" that most people seem to experience in their lives and spirituality is one way on filling the void.

CHAPTER 12

YOU MUST BE DISCIPLINED

Synopsis

Attaining spiritual discipline ensures the communication channel between man and the divine power remains open and accessible. It also helps to keep the focus of God also referred to as the said divine power.

Not to be misunderstood, being spiritually disciplined does not necessarily make an individual a spiritual person or a holy person; it just makes the individual's desire more intense to be aware of God's love for human kind.

Be Dedicated

Being spiritually disciplined encourages the individual to entrust their life into God's hand and be confident that all will be well. When this surrender is practiced regularly and completely, a habit if formed which in turn causes the confidence to increase in leaps and bounds in leaving everything to God, knowing that this divine power only wants the best for each individual being.

Spiritual discipline helps to ensure the relationship with God and man is in good working order and this helps to develop an intimacy between the two beings.

It does not however at any time promise total and complete bliss in cultivating this relationship although the peace factor gained is many folds.

In trying to understand the importance of discipline, one must first acknowledge that this spiritual discipline is a tool that helps to connect the physical body and mind with the inner spiritual inner man which in turn in deeply connected to God.

When this happens a lot changes in the mind's eye, and a whole other world of awareness opens up. Spiritual discipline helps the individual look upon his or her life from a spiritual perspective, and make the necessary changes to be in line with God's ways. Knowing that there is a mighty and divine power which is all knowing, guiding the individual's life further encourages people to pursue this form of discipline.

CHAPTER 13

LEARN HOW TO FORGIVE

Synopsis

Holding a grudge is both mentally and physically unhealthy. However learning to forgive on the other hand may sometimes be easier said than done. In order to preserve both the mental and physical health of an individual all efforts must be made to address the issue of forgiveness.

Get Over It

Depending on the hurt inflicted, the expectancy of forgiveness may indeed be difficult but not impossible. This is indeed good news for those struggling with letting go and forgiving.

Perhaps the first step would be the ability to forgive oneself of all wrong doing whether justified or not. In being able to forgive one's self then the person is ready and open to broach the subject of forgiving the offending party.

Most experts insist that the sooner the individual practices forgiveness and lets go of the problem the sooner the healing process can begin.

This also has an impact on the health of the individual bearing the grudge. The chemical changes that occur in the body are not healthy and really quite negative. Thus the urgency to reinstate the balance within the body by forgiving quickly.

The point to bear in mind is that the mistake cannot be undone, and therefore it is in the past, while the future does not have to live with the reminder of the mistake, if forgiveness is practiced.

Learning to forgive also reminds the person to avoid making the same mistake that lead to the cause of the pain. It gives the individual the presence of mind to walk away before any damage is done because now the individual has the strength and wisdom to do so. Not forgiving keeps the individual trapped and constantly being reminded of the painful memories of the past. Practicing forgiveness opens the door to a new way of thinking.

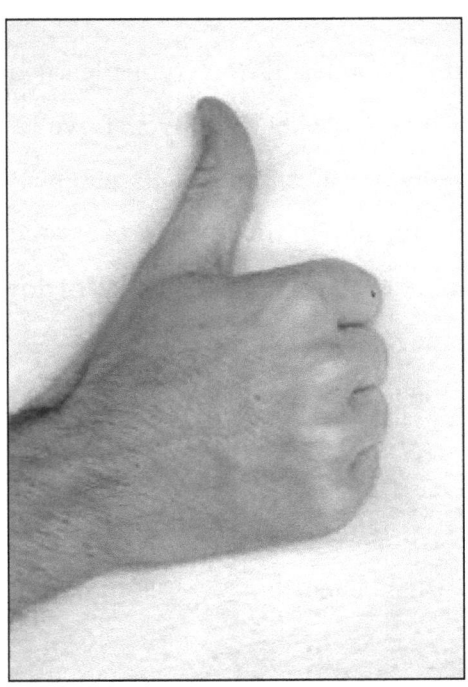

CHAPTER 14

LEARN HOW TO LIVE IN A STATE OF LOVE

Synopsis

Life would be wonderful if everyone learned to live by one rule only, and that rule being love. Love everything and everyone no matter what, simple in its essence but extremely hard to put to practice in reality. If everyone can learn to exchange a life of fear and pain for a life of love, many good things can be achieved.

Kinder

Most people look to the afterlife as being the perfect place on existence and try to work towards being able to attain the promise of this goal. However it has been proven that happiness can be found and kept consistent in this life too.

To get to this desired state to comfort, one must be able to consciously change any negative mind set with the specific intentions of living in self love, self trust, and total peace. All this takes considerable practice in facing the negative and making the effort to change the less that happy situation into a more acceptable level of joy.

Some basic points to note while on the quest to live in a state of love are as follows:

- Live for the now. Learn to enjoy each moment as if it was the last moment to have. This enables the individual to slow down and actually appreciate those around and be less critical as time is short.

- Value the important things life. Love those around consciously and with abandon and not withhold anything.

- Taking comfort in the divine power from within that is love and thus the ability to love unconditionally is possible.

- Keep the mind centered and focus to always be mindful of any negative elements that might creep into the thought process.

- Having loving thoughts and imaginations.

- Listening to calm and soothing music always unleashes the love from within which can identify with the beauty of sound.

- In listening to the inner voice and trusting it completely allows the individual to be less stressful and more relaxed and able to attract and reflect live.

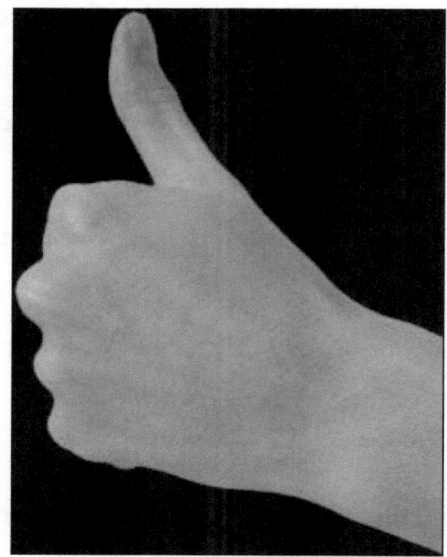

CHAPTER 15

HOW TO HEIGHTEN
YOUR SPIRITUAL CONNECTIONS

Synopsis

Spiritual connection can be view as being more aware of ourselves and everything around. Being spiritually connected allows us the luxury of being able to harness the positive energy to benefit all, which in turn creates a harmonious balance in body and mind.

Connecting

Being spiritually connected helps to strengthen many areas in an individual's life, such family relationships, community relationships, religion, health, and many others. The positive energy gained from heightened spirituality is what enables these things to take place.

Here are some ways to help heighten one's spiritual connections:

- Spending some quite time to meditate and pray is a good way to start the process of being spiritually connected. This allows foe the mind and body to seek and be aware of one's surroundings and thus have a clearer view of what is going on.

- Spending time interacting with like minded people. This is not only healthy but also builds relationships that can give positive mental and physical reinforcements.

- Set aside time to learn new things. In growing the mind, the rest of an individual's world grows along and the benefits of new things learnt are always useful.

- Having alone time is another very important factor to working towards spiritual connection. Taking this time to reboot and reflect is beneficial to both body and mind.

- Not surprisingly the encouragement of keeping a good exercise regiment and diet is also equally important. If the body and mind are at its optimum, everything other aspects of life becomes easier to connect to.

- Taking time to help others in a voluntary capacity helps to feed the inner man while the outwards benefits are the ability to be more compassionate towards others.

- Loving life is important too. Being able to simply have fun with abandon releases the positive energy that is the product of being spiritually connected.

CHAPTER 16

USING AROMATHERAPY

Synopsis

It is believed and scientifically proved by some quarters that all elements work on the basis of vibrations. Having put this point forth, it is interesting to discover that essential oils when used in aromatherapy also have similar vibration techniques that harness and create positive energy. Thus the use of aromatherapy in spiritual connecting has certain links.

Scent

Those who are familiar with this theory attest to the changes in energy when the use of aromatherapy is practiced. Among the claims made are that the vibrating higher frequency not only draws positive energy but also resonates this energy, while positive affecting all things around. This positive energy is so powerful that it can be used to shift the negative energy.

One does not have to be an expert in aromatherapy to know that scents effect the human body and mind distinctly. These scents are able to invoke emotions, memories, and even visions.

A lot of spiritual practices involve the use of aromatherapy style rituals. As mentioned, these uses of aromatherapy causes high frequency vibrations, and this enables the individual to connect with the inner self and experience total oneness with body and mind, keeping both well balanced in harmony.

Once the spiritual connection is established and easily maintained, many corresponding uses can be derived from using aromatherapy, such as complete oneness in thought, intent and purpose.

Purification rituals and healing processes, blending prayers with affirmations, mediations at a higher and more concentrated level and many others.

Before the medical world endorsed this type of process for assisting in the healing process or for keeping illnesses at bay, the aromatherapy use for spiritual purposes was prevalent in most ancient cultures. The connection and energy emitted and harnessed has its own unique elements of providing the necessary benefits to those seeking spiritual connections for healing or even for the general state of peace in both body and mind.

CHAPTER 17

USING CRYSTALS

Synopsis

Some would say crystals have a mysterious aura and power about them. The use of crystals dates back to ancient times where its uses varied, ranging from harnessing energy to healing.

It's a popular belief that these crystals were even used to help construct the enormously gigantic structures of the ancient past. Many cultures even today widely practice the use of crystals to achieve an aura of spirituality.

Crystals

The use of crystals in the process of attaining spirituality have been known to provide its user with certain elements like creativity, inspiration, knowledge, intuition which in turn produces a higher level of wisdom, enlightenment of the inner life, love, and peace just to name a few benefits.

Here is a list of the more popular crystals that are used for its various beneficial reasons:

- *Amethyst* – this crystal is known for its healing properties and helps in enhancing psychic awareness and imagery.

- *Bloodstone* – helps an individual stick to diet plans and curbs appetites.

- *Citrine* – a wonderful stone that can assist in manifesting one's goals. Also keeps the individual cheerful, attracts abundance and power.

- *Diamond* – is known as the stone of innocence which denotes purity.

- *Jade* – is used as a tool for learning to accept the difficult aspects in life.

- *Moonstone* – enhances intuitive sensitivity and the ability to except any new changes.

- *Opal* – is considered to be one of the seven sacred stones of the Cherokee.

- *Ruby* – it brings love, confidence, loyalty, and courage which strengthen the physical and emotional heart.

- *Sapphire* – this stone comes in many pretty colors and has healing and spiritual properties

- *Topaz* – allows an individual to have a practical and focused outlook in life.

- *Turquoise* – is wonderful for drawing out negative vibrations

- *White opal* – a great charging tool because it energizes and thus help the individual to get more things done.

CHAPTER 18

EMOTIONAL HEALING WITH REFLEXOLOGY

Synopsis

Very few people would turn down an opportunity to be on the receiving end of a wonderful session of a relaxing foot massage.

Beneficial to both the receiver and the giver, especially when practiced by loved ones, this form of therapy not only gives of one's own time but also build compassion, and a caring attitude in the giver. These, along with the various benefits of addressing the various reflex points, are incomparably priceless.

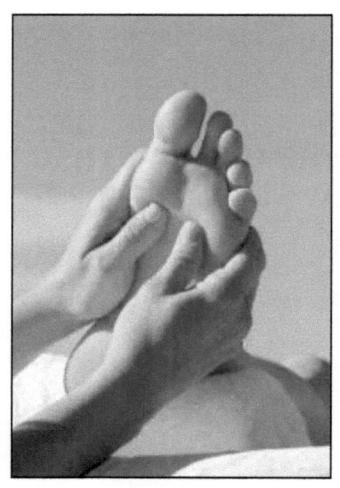

Massage

The practice of applying pressure to certain points while stretching to stimulate corresponding areas in the body system creates and promotes healing. The most sought after element is to obtain relief from stress both emotionally and physically.

Even if the technique used is not purely form a reflexologist stand point, the benefits to impart some form of emotional balance is phenomenal. In encouraging the body to heal itself, the emotional strain the problem put on the mind is thus eased and balance is restored.

It has been proven time and again that most physical problems are somehow linked or brought on by the poor emotional state of an individual. Therefore in addressing the emotional imbalance half the battle is won. There are specific links to various organs in the body such as anger which is literally linked to the liver, grief and sadness is linked to the lungs while fear is linked to the kidneys and so on.

All this translates to various emotional stress conditions like tension which is the lead cause of headaches, fear brings on difficulty in breathing, and nervousness causes sweaty palms. Emotional healing goes a long way in addressing any physical problem has long been established. Another scientifically established fact is that each organ in the human body responds and emits vibration frequencies which are connected to the emotion it draws from which has the same corresponding vibrations.

CHAPTER 19

KNOW THAT YOU DESERVE HEALING

Synopsis

Everyone deserves all the attention possible in order to start the healing process. Healing is for everyone but there are some people who genuinely believe that the healing process is not for them or that they are undeserving of it. Some even believe that the negative medical or mental problem is so far gone that that it is not possible to treat the condition and so they don't even try.

You Merit This

A big part of the problem lies in the belief levels of the individual, which effects the positive manifestation of the desired effect. Some of the mindset that needs to be addressed and changed in order for the healing process to begin is acknowledging the problem, realizing that it can be overcome and being confident that the healing is deserving. When these are accepted then the healing process can begin.

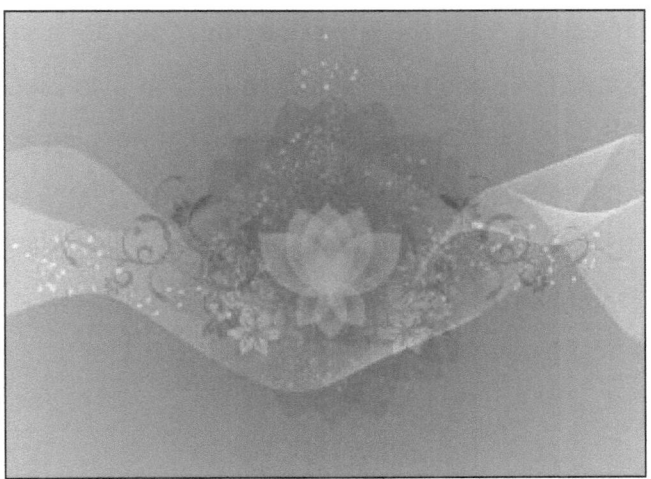

Unfortunately there are more reasons than not as to why people generally fail to accept that healing is for them and it is possible to accomplish complete healing. Feelings like ridicule or pressure from family tired of fighting and seeing no positive break throughs, seeking various forms of healing without giving it the proper duration to make an impact, costly styles and tools, contracting difficult to cure conditions and lack of informed support.

Fortunately there are people who believe in the healing process that not necessarily have to involve pharmaceutical medications. These people can help those in need to gain the confidence to embark on the healing journey.

In releasing and changing the mind set to accept that healing is available and deserved the body can then process this information and start to address the chemical imbalanced which is a huge part of the healing process. When the mind is ready for the positive energy the body generates in this process, the balance is gradually restored and this results in the restoration to optimum health conditions.

Wrapping Up

People who have the advantage of being spiritually connected are much happier people as they are able to deal with outer turbulences better than those without the essence of spirituality.

They are completely aware and dependant on this spiritual "help" to give them relief and sound thinking in any given situation. Without spiritual direction it is often difficult to have a goal to work towards and certainly hard to keep focused when things start looking difficult or negative.

Spirituality may be seen as being distinct from religion. Assorted world religions have proposed assorted philosophies and belief systems about the nature of a God and humanity's kinship with it. Spirituality, on the other hand, refers to the basic experience behind these assorted viewpoints.

It's an experience involving an awareness of and relationship with something that exceeds your personal self as well as the mortal order of things. This "something" has been given assorted names and delineated in ways that are too many to count. You are able to decide to define what that means for yourself in whatsoever way feels most suited.

Your own sense of a God may be as abstract as "cosmic consciousness" or as earthy as the beauty of the ocean or mountains. Even if you regard yourself an agnostic or atheist, you might get a sense of inspiration from taking a walk in the forest or studying a beautiful sunset. Or a small youngster's smile may give you a special sense of delight.

Whatever the case embark on spiritual healing journey.

Printed by Libri Plureos GmbH in Hamburg, Germany